GW00361170

TABLE GRACES

Compiled by Lois L. Kaufman

Design by Arlene Greco

PETER PAUPER PRESS, INC.
WHITE PLAINS, NEW YORK

For Paul Simpson McElroy,
who wrote and compiled many of
the graces in this book

Copyright © 1997
Peter Pauper Press, Inc.
202 Mamaroneck Avenue
White Plains, NY 10601
ISBN 0-88088-821-0
Printed in China
7 6 5 4 3 2

TABLE GRACES

*T*hank you

for the

food we eat...

For food and drink and happy days,

Accept our gratitude and praise;

In serving others, Lord, may we

Repay in part our debt to Thee.

Give me a good digestion, Lord,

And also something to digest;

Give me a healthy body, Lord,

With sense to keep it at its best.

Found in Chester Cathedral, England

Thou art great and Thou art good,

And we thank Thee for this food;

By Thy hands will we be fed,

Give us, Lord, our daily bread.

Amen.

The eyes of all look hopefully to you, O Lord. And you give them their food in due season. You open your hand and fill every living creature with blessing.

*D*ear Lord, we thank you for the bounty of this, your table. And, as we accept your gifts, help us to be accepting of others.

Kent F. Warner

$\mathcal{B}$e present at our table, Lord,

Be here and everywhere adored.

Thy creatures bless, and grant that we

May feast in paradise with Thee.

John Wesley

$\mathcal{T}$hank you

for the friends

we meet…

*G*od is great and God is good,

And we thank Him for this food.

By His hand must all be fed;

Give us, Lord, our daily bread.

The Hampton Grace

$\mathcal{G}$ive us grateful hearts, our
Father, for all thy mercies, and
make us mindful of the needs
of others.

Book of Common Prayer

$\mathcal{F}$or each new morning with

　　its light…

For rest and shelter of the night,

For health and food, for love

　　and friends,

For everything Thy goodness sends.

Ralph Waldo Emerson

*O*ur Father, by whose hand we are fed, we bless Thee for this living bread. Amen.

*B*e present at our table, Lord;

Be here and everywhere adored.

Thy children bless, and grant

that we

May feast in fellowship with Thee.

Isaac Watts

*N*ow thank we all our God,

With heart and hand and voices

Who wondrous things hath done,

In whom His world rejoices.

Catherine Winkworth

$\mathcal{T}$hank you God,

For food so good,

Lord help us do

The things we should.

O God, our Father, who giveth food for the body and truth for the mind; so enlighten and nourish us that we may grow wise and strong to do Thy will.

*T*hank you

for our work

and play...

Thank you, God, for milk and bread

And other things so good.

Thank you, God, for those who help

To grow and cook our food.

*F*or health and strength

And daily bread

We praise Thy name, O Lord.

(Sung as a round)

For fruit and milk

For bread and meat,

For all this food

So good to eat–

We thank you, God. Amen

$\mathcal{T}$hank you, O God, so good,

For today's bread.

Thank you for watching over us,

Thank you for your love.

*W*e thank Thee, Lord, for happy
hearts,

For rain and sunny weather.

We thank Thee, Lord, for this our
food,

And that we are together.

*A*ll things bright and beautiful.

All creatures great and small,

All things wise and wonderful:

The Lord God made them all.

*T*hank you,

God, for a

happy day.

*O*ur Father, we are grateful for
this family, who hand in hand
form one unbroken circle. Help
us to do Thy will, as caring
individuals and as a loving family.

Amen.

For this new morning and

    its light,

For rest and shelter of the night,

For health and food, for love and

    friends,

For every gift His goodness sends,

I thank Thee, gracious Lord. Amen.

Father for this morning

    (noonday, evening) meal

We would speak the praise we feel.

Health and strength we ask

    of Thee,

Help us, Lord, to faithful be.

P raised be Thou

O Lord our God,

Ruler of the world,

Who causes the earth to yield

food for all.

O God, we thank Thee for this food: as we live by Thy bounty, may we live continually to Thy praise.

*L*ord, place Thy blessing upon us
as we prepare to receive this food.
We thank Thee for new strength,
in God's name. Amen.

*T*hank you

for the world

so sweet...

*W*e thank Thee, our heavenly
Father, for Thy care over us
and pray that Thou wilt bless
this food to our use.

*F*ather in heaven, sustain our
bodies with this food, our hearts
with true friendship, and our souls
with Thy truth.

*B*less us, O Lord, and these Thy
gifts, which we are about to
receive from Thy bounty.

T hanks be to Thee,
O Lord, for these and all
the blessings so generously
provided.

For daily bread, for all things
    good,
For life and health, for this our food,
For each good gift Thy grace
    imparts,
We thank Thee, Lord, with humble
    hearts.

Clifford Wesley Collins

O God, make us able

For all that's on the table! Amen.

Eire

This food, which Thou has already blessed in the giving, do Thou further bless in our partaking, that it may redound to Thy glory. Amen.

We thank Thee, God, for milk
and bread
And all our daily food;
These gifts remind us day by day,
Our Father, Thou art good.

Herman J. Sweet

*T*hank you

for the food

we eat...

*F*ather, we thank Thee for this

    food,

For all the blessings Thou dost

    give;

Strengthen our bodies and our

    souls,

And let us for Thy service live.

O God, bless our home, our family, friends, and neighbors, and give us thankful hearts for all Thy mercies.

*O*ur Father, we bless Thee for this food and for all expressions of Thy goodness to us. Give us grace ever to do Thy will.

$\mathcal{B}$lessed art Thou, King of the Universe, who bringest forth food from the earth.

O ur Father, let the spirit of
gratitude so prevail in our hearts
that we may manifest Thy spirit
in our lives.

W. B. Slack

For this our daily bread, and for every good gift which cometh down from Thee, we bless Thy holy name.

$\mathcal{S}$anctify, O Lord, we beseech Thee, this food to our use, and us to Thy service, and make us truly thankful for all these mercies.

With heart as well as lips,

    dear God,

We thank you for this food;

For countless other blessings too,

We offer gratitude.

Gracious Giver of all good,

Thee we thank for rest and food.

Grant that all we do or say

In Thy service be this day.

$\mathcal{A}$ t this table, Lord, we ask

That Thou wilt be our guest.

We thank Thee, Father, for this
food,

And may we all be blest.

We're thankful for the many
   things
Our heavenly Father sends:
For love and faith and strength
   and health,
For home and food and friends.

Give us grateful hearts, our
Father, for all Thy mercies, and
make us mindful of the needs
of others.

*T*hank you

for the birds

that sing.

*F*or these and all His blessings

may God's holy name be praised.

*B*less, O Lord, these gifts to our

use and ourselves to Thy service.

$\mathcal{L}$ord, Thou has not need of our thanks, but we have daily need to remind ourselves of our obligation unto Thee. For all Thy mercies make us ever truly grateful.

To God who gives us daily bread

A thankful song we raise,

And pray that He who sends

    us food

Will fill our hearts with praise.

Mary Rumsey

*F*or what we are about to receive, O Lord, make us truly grateful. Amen.

*T*ransform this food into life,

O God, and transform that life

into useful service of Thee. Amen.

Lord, gratitude we offer all who
labor that we may be fed;
O dignify our toil for them,
Bring kinship through our daily
bread.

Olive Haskins

*H*eavenly Father, be our Guest;

Our morning joy, our evening

rest;

And with our daily bread impart

Thy love and peace to every

heart.

L ord, make us truly grateful for the blessings of this day, and keep us Thine evermore.

$\mathcal{T}$hou has given so much to us, give one thing more: a grateful heart.

*D*ear Lord, we thank you for all the material and spiritual blessings that you shower on us. Help us to share all that we have with those who are less fortunate.

Kent F. Warner

Give us Lord, a bit o' sun,

A bit o' work and a bit o' fun;

Give us all in the struggle and

   sputter

Our daily bread and a bit o' butter.

On the wall of an old inn,
Lancaster, England

$\mathcal{T}$hank you,

God,

for everything.

Amen.

E. Rutter Leatham

$\mathcal{W}$e thank Thee, heavenly Father,

For every earthly good.

For life, for health, for shelter,

And for our daily food.

*H*eavenly Father, Thou hast given us our daily bread. Out of our abundance may we remember those of Thy children who cry aloud to Thee for bread–but have it not.

*L*et Thy peace and blessing descend upon us as we take of Thy bounty. Fill our hearts with praise toward Thee and love toward our fellowmen.

*G*od, bless this food to our use,

and bless our lives to Thy service,

and make us in our blessings ever

mindful of the needs of others.

O God our Father, be Thou the Unseen Guest at our table, and fill our hearts with Thy love.

$\mathscr{K}$eep us ever humble, Lord, that we may be the ready recipients of Thy goodness. Deliver us from pride and wickedness, and supply our wants. Amen.

*C*hildren come in many colors

They live in different lands

But one God watches over all

We're safe in God's sure hands.

                        Amen.

Some hae meat and canna eat,

And some would eat that want it;

But we hae meat, and we can eat,

Sae let the Lord be thankit.

Robert Burns

$\mathcal{G}$racious Father, we give thanks
to Thee for the gifts we have
enjoyed through Thy bountiful
goodness.

*T*hank you for the food we eat;

Thank you for the friends we meet;

Thank you for our work and play;

Thank you, God, for a happy day.

$\mathcal{T}$hank you for the world so

sweet,

Thank you for the foods we eat,

Thank you for the birds that sing.

Thank you, God, for everything.

Amen.

E. Rutter Leatham